Respect

by Matthew Dylan

RAINTREE
STECK-VAUGHN
PUBLISHERS

A Harcourt Company

Austin   New York
www.raintreesteckvaughn.com

Published by Raintree Steck-Vaughn Publishers, an imprint of Steck-Vaughn Company.

Library of Congress Cataloging-in-Publication Data is available upon request.

ISBN: 0-7398-5780-0

Printed and bound in China
1 2 3 4 5 6 7 8 9 10   05 04 03 02

A Creative Media Applications, Inc. Production

Photo Credits:
AP/Wide World Photographs: Cover
AP/Wide World Photographs: Pages 5, 6, 7, 9, 10, 11, 13, 15, 16, 17, 18, 19, 20, 21, 22, 23, 25, 26, 27

Editor: Matt Levine
Indexer: Joan Verniero
Design and Production: Alan Barnett, Inc.
Photo Research: Yvette Reyes

Contents

"I have a dream that my four children will one day live in a nation where they will not be judged by the color of their skin but by the content of their character."

—Dr. Martin Luther King, Jr., civil rights leader and winner of the Nobel Peace Prize

The dictionary says that respect is "high or special regard" for someone or something. You can show respect through courtesy. However, respect goes beyond courtesy. Respect means that you treat others the way that you would like to be treated by them. This is sometimes called the Golden Rule.

There are many forms of respect. Respect is an important part of how you relate to people. Respect means treating everyone with dignity. All people deserve respect regardless of their **gender,** race, religion, or ability. In addition, respect for property, your country, and ideas are all American **ideals.**

Respect for each person's rights is very important in this country. Dr. Martin Luther King, Jr., believed that everyone should be treated with respect. In his famous "I Have a Dream" speech, he said that the rights of all Americans must be respected for the United States to be free.

It is very hard to respect someone if he or she does not respect you. Also, it is hard for others to respect you if you do not show them respect. Showing respect for others and being respected is the basis of friendship.

Dr. Martin Luther King Jr. talks to marchers during his "I Have a Dream" speech at the Lincoln Memorial in Washington, D.C., on August 28, 1963.

The United States is a place where every person expects to be treated with respect. However, this was not always true. Until certain laws were changed, some Americans were not given the respect that they deserved.

In some parts of the United States, blacks and whites

Rosa Parks is fingerprinted by Deputy Sheriff D.H. Lackey in Montgomery, Alabama, on February 22, 1956, two months after refusing to give up her seat on a bus for a white person.

were not treated equally. They could not live in the same neighborhoods. They could not attend the same schools. Separation of people based on race is one type of **segregation.** Segregation was allowed in some parts

This is the inside of the bus on which Rosa Parks refused to give up her seat in 1955.

of the United States until the 1960s. Segregation meant that some people were not shown the respect that they deserved as Americans.

In Montgomery, Alabama, blacks were expected to give up their seats on the bus to white people. On December 1, 1955, a young black woman named Rosa Parks was on a bus. A white man boarded and expected to take her seat. Parks refused to give it up. She demanded that the other passengers respect her right to keep her seat.

Parks was arrested and fined for standing up for her rights. Others joined her cause. Blacks, as well as white supporters, took her case to the highest court, the United States Supreme Court. A year later, the Supreme Court ruled that Montgomery's bus segregation laws were illegal. This was a big step toward ending segregation and gaining respect for all Americans.

Self-respect means holding yourself in high regard. It is sometimes called self-esteem. This does not mean that you think you are better than others. It means that you care for yourself as a person, and that you believe you are a worthwhile human being. All other forms of respect are impossible without self-respect.

You show respect for yourself in many ways. You respect your body by eating right, exercising, bathing, brushing your teeth, and visiting the doctor. You respect your intelligence by working hard in school, reading, and

S.A.F.E. K.I.D.S.

A group of teenagers in Brooklyn, New York, realized their friends needed to build self-esteem for themselves. These teenagers started S.A.F.E. K.I.D.S. (Safe Alternatives For Empowering Kids In Disadvantaged Situations). This group helped them avoid self-destructive behaviors. They organized an annual street festival where kids perform. They publish a magazine. At the S.A.F.E. K.I.D.S. teen center, kids help each other gain self-esteem.

*These West Iredale Middle School seventh graders
in Statesville, North Carolina, build self-esteem
by working together on a reading project.*

completing your homework.

Showing self-respect is different for each person. Sometimes it is necessary to stand up for yourself. It is important to say what you think is right. In Montgomery, Alabama, Rosa Parks showed courage by demanding respect on the bus. You also can show courage by taking care of yourself. In this way you earn self-respect and the respect of others.

Anton Hopkins, 7, holds a candle during the Stop the Hate, Stop the Violence interfaith rally at Columbus City Hall in Indiana.

Respect for the differences of others is called **tolerance.** Everyone is different, but all people share the right to be respected. Tolerance is an important American value. However, sometimes Americans have been treated with intolerance. Intolerance is a lack of respect for people who are different from you.

Intolerance may happen because someone belongs to a different race. It may happen because someone has different beliefs or abilities. Intolerance can happen because another person is the opposite gender.

Disliking or showing disrespect for someone because he or she is different is called **prejudice.** Prejudice is the opposite of tolerance. When people are treated unequally because of their differences, it is called **discrimination.**

During the 1950s and 1960s, black Americans fought against discrimination. Their struggle was called the civil rights movement. Laws that allowed discrimination were changed. Other groups in the United States and throughout the world have fought for respect also. Many of these struggles have changed people's attitudes in a positive way.

Today, intolerance still exists. One way to fight against intolerance is to show respect for everyone. When you meet someone who is different from you, imagine what it might feel like to be that person. Listen carefully to what he or she has to say. Remember that all people have the right to be respected for who they are.

Jihan Haji, 10, center, wears a traditional Kurdish head covering as she and other fourth and fifth graders participate in a program honoring students' differences. This Bremerton, Washington, program teaches tolerance.

Courtesy simply means being polite. This may seem like an old-fashioned idea. Some people believe that there is little need for courtesy today. That is wrong. Courtesy is a form of respect. Most people expect to be treated politely. Some ways of showing respect or courtesy have changed since your parents were young. However, many basic rules of courtesy have not changed. For example, when you meet someone, it is courteous to say, "Hello."

Courtesy helps people communicate with one another and form friendships. Courtesy includes being helpful,

Some Rules of School Courtesy

- Walk on the right side of the hallway without blocking traffic.
- Go to the end of the line when others are waiting.
- Arrive on time to class, and wait until you are dismissed to leave.
- Throw your trash in the trash containers.
- Do not call others names.
- Do not use bad language.

Rachel Strickland, 10, center, Lisa Luna, 10, right, and other students in a fifth-grade class raise their hands politely to give an answer during a group lesson.

kind, and polite to all people. Many schools have rules of basic courtesy. These rules help students get along in and out of the classroom.

One way to show respect to others is to speak courteously. This is especially important when you speak to adults. The "polite" words that you learned when you were very young still work. Saying "please" and "thank you" show respect and show that you are a courteous person. When you are courteous, others will be courteous to you in return.

Lack of respect for the environment has caused much damage. As a result many water sources are polluted. Earth's rain forests are being destroyed. However, many young people have shown great respect for Earth. In addition, they are helping others learn to respect it.

Recently President George W. Bush presented the President's Environmental Youth Awards. These awards honor students who complete projects that show great respect and caring for the environment. The awards were presented at a ceremony at the White House on

President's Environmental Youth Award

Award winners completed projects that

- started a trash cleanup club in their school.
- established a battery recycling program to help prevent pollution.
- set up a place to dispose of oil and other petroleum products.
- adopted wetlands and protected the animals and plants that live there.

Fifth-grader Clayton Walker looks for misplaced recyclables between lunch periods at Oak Grove School in Graton, California. Leftover food is saved for local farmers to use as pig feed.

April 24, 2001. President Bush said, "It's our young who are…cleaning up [the] environment."

You do not have to win an award from the president to show respect for the environment. Students throughout the country join cleanup programs and other events to help the environment. Simple acts can show great respect for the environment. Throw your trash in the wastebasket. Turn off unnecessary lights. Do not waste water. These things show that you respect Earth.

For most of U.S. history, women did not receive the same respect as men. Women could not vote in this country until 1920. This idea seems strange today. Now women vote in greater numbers than men. In addition, many women are elected to jobs in the government.

In the past, women often could not get the same jobs as men. Ida May Phillips was one of the first women to demand workplace equality. She applied for a job in a factory in Florida. The factory said that she could not

Hundreds of men and women hand-stitch the leather covers on baseballs at the Rawlings baseball factory. At one time women could not get the same jobs as men.

San Francisco Bay Area Girl Scout troops take off on a 2,000-meter run to kick off "GirlSports 2000," a sports program for girls ages 5 to 17. Women now have more team sports choices than they did years ago.

have the job because she was a woman with small children. Phillips fought for the job all the way to the United States Supreme Court. On January 25, 1971, the court ruled that employers could not discriminate on the basis of gender. Phillips won her job.

The right to education is very important for gaining respect. In 1974 the U.S. Congress passed new laws about education. One new law was Title IX. This law says that schools must offer equal programs to men and women. As a result, more scholarships are now offered to women.

In sports most coaches and many athletes say that
winning is not everything. They say that being a good
sport is more important than winning.

Good **sportsmanship** means showing respect for the
game, the other players and officials. Respect for the
game begins with following the rules. Even when you

*Good sports show respect for the other team. Detroit Red Wings
goalie Chris Osgood is congratulated by the St. Louis Blues'
Wayne Gretzky after the Red Wings beat the Blues.*

disagree with a rule, it is important to respect it.

Playing hard and trying to win do not prevent you from respecting the other team. Heckling or name-calling shows disrespect for the opposing players. Congratulating the other side whether you win or lose shows respect for their efforts. Celebrating when you win or score is a normal reaction. Cheer for your teammates. However, be aware that celebrating too much might be inconsiderate and disrespectful. If you show respect for your opponents, they should show respect for you.

Stanford University guards Lindsey Yamasaki, left, and Kelley Suminski cheer on the team in the final minutes of the second half against Arizona.

Respect for officials is very important in every sport. Officials do their best to make the correct calls every time. However, they are human. They make mistakes, just like players. It is easy to show respect for an official when the call goes your way. You can show true respect by behaving respectfully if a call goes against you.

Respect in sports goes beyond the sidelines. Parents and other spectators owe the players respect. People who yell at the players, coaches, and officials show disrespect for them and a lack of self-respect, as well.

Speed skater Karin van Tongeren, right, of the Netherlands receives her silver medal for the 500-meter speed-skating event during the Special Olympic World Winter Games in 2001.

Every four years, a very special Olympics competition is held. This competition is not the Olympics that most people know. It is the Special Olympics. The athletes in the Special Olympics compete for medals. They train hard for their events. However, Special Olympics athletes are competing for more than medals. They are competing for respect. Special Olympics athletes face more than physical challenges. They are also mentally challenged.

In 1960 the Special Olympics got its start when Eunice Kennedy Shriver began a day camp for mentally retarded children. She believed that sports training and competition would help these children build self-esteem. The program grew quickly to include Olympic-style events. The Special Olympics tries to help children and adults with mental retardation to improve their skills. In addition these athletes gain self-respect and show great courage.

Today, Special Olympics athletes compete throughout the United States and 150 other countries. Every four years, these athletes come together for the Special Olympics World Games. More than one million athletes train and compete in 26 different summer and winter sports. They try to win medals in sports such as cycling, skiing, power lifting, soccer, and basketball. These events provide opportunities for people with mental retardation to show that they deserve the same respect as others.

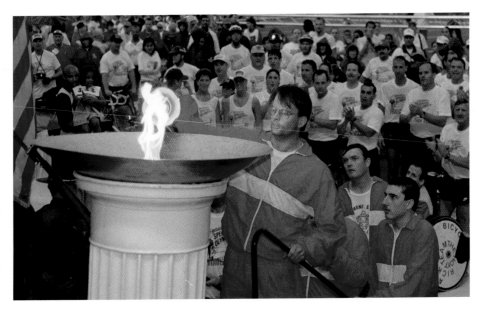

Special Olympics torchbearer and volleyball team member Tim Goodale lights the Flame of Hope during opening ceremonies at the 26th Annual Massachusetts Special Olympics Summer Games.

Respect for Authority

People who carry out the laws and rules of the government have authority. Everyone should respect people in authority. They help people live together. They make the world safer. They are often leaders.

In sports the coach and the officials have authority. Without their authority the game could not be played. Respect for their authority allows the players to stay within the rules and have a fair game. The police represent authority in cities and towns. They enforce the laws that keep people safe and allow everyone to live together. Respecting the authority of the police is an important American value.

Officers salute the flag at the Vermont Police Day ceremony at the statehouse in Montpelier, Vermont.

Philadelphia principal Carolyn James Weeks, center, is seen with students Raymond Williams, left, and India Stephens-Bey.

Your parents are the authorities at home. They enforce family rules that help you to grow up to be a good person. At school the teachers and principal are the authorities. They make rules and treat students fairly. The rules help make school a safe place. School rules also help make school a good place to learn.

You show respect for authority by listening and following directions. Respect for authority shows respect for others and it shows self-respect. One day you will be in a position of authority. Then you will expect others to respect you and follow your lead.

You have many things that belong to you. These things are your property. They include your clothes, toys, and schoolwork. You own these things. You have the right to expect that others will treat them with respect. Respect for your property means that it will not be taken without your permission. If you lend something to another person, it should be returned to you without damage.

Intellectual Property

In addition to things such as your toys and clothes, there is another type of property that deserves respect. This is **intellectual property.** Intellectual property is anything that you create, write, or make. This includes your homework, tests, or writing assignments. Respecting your intellectual property means that you do not allow others to pretend it is theirs or copy it. At the same time, you show respect for others' property by never presenting someone else's work as your own. This includes never copying directly from encyclopedias or other books.

Fifth-grade teacher Meg Nolan prepares her classroom for the new school year at Antheil Elementary School in Ewing, New Jersey. It is important for students to respect each other's property.

If someone accidentally damages your property, you should expect that person to fix or replace it. Respect for your property also shows respect for you.

It is important to treat other people's property with respect. You show respect for other people's property in the same way that they show respect for yours. This includes respecting school property and property in your community. Stay away from places you are not allowed to go. Do not misuse things that do not belong to you.

When you respect your own property, it shows others how you expect them to treat your things. Taking care of your clothes, toys, video games, and sports equipment shows your respect for these things and yourself.

When people share their ideas with others, it is important that the ideas are treated with respect. You can show respect by listening to what others have to say. Ideas should be judged on their merits. It is disrespectful to judge ideas based on prejudice. Respect for ideas is one of the most important traditions in a **democracy.**

In the late 18th century, a group of people living in North America had a new idea. They believed that a country could rule itself through democracy. In 1776, this idea and others formed the basis of a document called the Declaration of Independence. More than 200 years later, this country, which began with the Declaration of Independence, still exists. Among the most important ideas in the Declaration of Independence is that all people are created equal. If you believe this idea, then it follows that all people

This is a rare first printing of the Declaration of Independence, the cornerstone of American democracy.

Delegates to the United Nations share ideas.
These delegates show respect for each other by listening
and then voting for what they believe is right.

should be treated with respect.

The Constitution says that all Americans have the right
to speak their ideas freely. This is called "freedom of
speech." The Constitution does not require you to agree
with everyone's ideas. However, Americans must respect
each other's right to express their ideas. Freedom of speech
and respect for ideas are important American values.

Respect for Your Country

The Declaration of Independence and the Constitution protect certain rights. These rights make sure that every American is treated with respect. In a democracy it is also important for **citizens** to respect the government.

Respect for your country means that you obey the laws, vote, and stay informed about important issues. Of course you are free to speak out even when your opinions do not

The Peace Corps

In 1961 President John F. Kennedy said, "My fellow Americans: ask not what your country can do for you—ask what you can do for your country." The country had done much for all Americans. He asked Americans to show their respect for the United States by giving something back. Many young Americans responded by joining the Peace Corps. Peace Corps volunteers work in other countries to promote world peace and friendship. Since 1961 more than 163,000 Americans have become Peace Corps volunteers. This organization is respected throughout the world.

A sergeant faces the soldiers who report to him. Volunteering to join the armed forces is a great way to show respect for America.

agree with the government. However, you can show respect for your country by expressing your opinions in the right ways. These include **debating** ideas and, most importantly, voting.

There are other ways to show respect for your country. You can stand when the national anthem is played. Reciting the Pledge of Allegiance in school also shows respect for your country.

People who join the Armed Forces respect their country by serving it. People who help others by volunteering their time show respect for their fellow Americans. Helping others who are less fortunate is one way that many students show respect. America is more than just the government. It is all the people who make up the United States. When you show respect for other Americans, you show respect for your country.

Glossary

Citizen: A member of a country, nation, city, or town

Debate: To consider a question or issue by discussing opposing points of view

Democracy: A nation that has a government run by its citizens

Discrimination: Unfair or unequal treatment of others

Gender: A person's sexual identity, male or female

Ideal: A standard or model of perfection or excellence

Intellectual property: Original creative work, such as writing, art, computer programs, and inventions

Prejudice: Judgement of people without all the facts

Segregation: Forced separation of people in order to practice discrimination

Sportsmanship: Playing fair and following the rules

Tolerance: Recognizing and respecting the beliefs or practices of others

James, Elizabeth. *Social Smarts: Modern Manners for Today's Kids.* New York: Clarion Books, 1996.
This is a book of advice on how to deal with various issues of etiquette, including introductions, school dances, vacations, meals, parties, bereaved friends, and many others.

Jeffers, Susan. *Brother Eagle, Sister Sky.* New York: Dial, 1991.
This book is adapted from a Native American tale. It is a story about respect for the environment.

Fleischman, S.J. *The Whipping Boy.* Mahwah, NJ: Troll, 1987.
In this story, Prince Brat learns about the power of respect and kindness from an orphan named Jeremy.

www.epa.gov/kids/
This site, the U.S. EPA Explorers' Club, is for kids interested in protecting and respecting the environment.

Index